HOW IT'S BUILT
CAR

by Becky Herrick

Illustrations by Richard Watson

Children's Press®
An imprint of Scholastic Inc.

Thanks to Don Sherman, independent automobile professional, for his role as content consultant for this book.

Thanks to Donna Lowich, Senior Information Specialist at the Christopher & Dana Reeve Foundation, for her insights into the daily lives of people who use wheelchairs.

Library of Congress Cataloging-in-Publication Data
Names: Herrick, Becky, author. | Watson, Richard, 1980– illustrator.
Title: How it's built. Car/by Becky Herrick; illustrations by Richard Watson.
Other titles: Car
Description: First edition. | New York, NY: Children's Press, an imprint of Scholastic Inc., 2022. | Includes index. |
    Audience: Ages 5–7 | Audience: Grades K–1 | Summary:
    "Narrative nonfiction with fictional characters who visit various work sites to find out how different structures
    are built. Full-color illustrations and photographs throughout"—Provided by publisher.
Identifiers: LCCN 2021029563 (print) | LCCN 2021029564 (ebook) | ISBN 9781338800173 (library binding) |
    ISBN 9781338800180 (paperback) | ISBN 9781338800197 (ebk)
Subjects: LCSH: Automobiles—Design and construction—Juvenile literature. | BISAC: JUVENILE NONFICTION/
    Technology/How Things Work–Are Made
Classification: LCC TL240 .H465 2022 (print) | LCC TL240 (ebook) | DDC 629.2/31—dc23
LC record available at https://lccn.loc.gov/2021029563
LC ebook record available at https://lccn.loc.gov/2021029564

10 9 8 7 6 5 4 3 2 1   22 23 24 25 26

Printed in the U.S.A.   113
First edition, 2022

Series produced by Spooky Cheetah Press
Book design by Maria Bergós, Book & Look
Page design by Kathleen Petelinsek, The Design Lab

Photos ©: back cover: Chris Ratcliffe/Bloomberg/Getty Images; 5 bottom left: Andrey Rudakov/Bloomberg/Getty Images; 5 bottom right: Chris Ratcliffe/ Bloomberg/Getty Images; 6 left: Motoring Picture Library/Alamy Images; 9 right background: Pgiam/Getty Images; 10 left: fStop Images GmbH/Alamy Images; 10 right: Jan Woitas/picture alliance/Getty Images; 11 top left: Sergiy Serdyuk/Alamy Images; 11 bottom left: Sandy Huffaker/Bloomberg/Getty Images; 14 left: Monty Rakusen/Cultura Creative RF/Alamy Images; 17 inset: Gary Cameron/Reuters/ Alamy Images; 18–19: Andrey Rudakov/Bloomberg/Getty Images; 19 inset: Ewing Galloway/UIG/Shutterstock; 20 top left: Monty Rakusen/Cultura Creative RF/Alamy Images; 20 top right: Friedrich Stark/Alamy Images; 21 top left: Chris Honeywell/ Alamy Images; 24–25: Sean Gallup/Getty Images; 26–27: Chris Ratcliffe/ Bloomberg/Getty Images; 28 top left: Nataliya Hora/Dreamstime; 28 bottom left: Andrey Rudakov/Bloomberg/Getty Images; 29 top left: Monty Rakusen/ Getty Images; 30 top left: NASA; 31 top left: Hammacher Schlemmer/Solent/ Shutterstock; 31 center right: David Paul Morris/Bloomberg/Getty Images.

All other photos © Shutterstock.

TABLE OF CONTENTS

• MEET THE JUNIOR ENGINEERS CLUB •

Sofia

Lucas

Kai

Nisha

Jacob

Zoe

These six friends love learning about
how things are built! This is their workshop.

Kai and Zoe found out how a car is built.
Now they are sharing what they learned!

It can take up to six years of planning to make a new car model. But when all the car's parts are ready, they can be put together in less than a day!

PROJECTS
HOUSE
CAR
BRIDGE
SKYSCRAPER
ROCKET
SAILBOAT

• LET'S BUILD A CAR! •

Hi! I am Kai, and this is my friend Zoe. We visited a car factory where my neighbor Laura works. Laura explained that cars range in size from small two-door cars to SUVs and pickup trucks. She said that cars can be powered in different ways.

A **gas car** is powered by a gasoline engine. It is also called a **conventional** car because it is what most people mean when they talk about a "car."

An **electric car** uses an electric motor instead of a gasoline engine. The motor is powered by energy stored onboard in batteries.

A **hybrid car** has a gasoline engine and an electric motor. Sometimes the vehicle uses just the gasoline engine. Sometimes it uses just the electric motor. Sometimes it uses both together!

The factory where I work makes cars with gasoline engines.

Laura told us that the first step in making a new car is coming up with the design. First, designers sketch what the car will look like. Then engineers decide how the car will be built and how it will work.

Car designers think about what will make a car work safely and well. They also think about what will look cool and what people will enjoy!

Or all the seats could spin around?

870

Next, the company makes prototypes of the car. These full-size working models are put through a lot of tests. Then any problems with the design can be fixed. Laura told us about some of the different kinds of tests.

Dummies, or big dolls, are used in **crash tests**. These tests help engineers see what would happen to the car and its passengers in an actual crash.

High-speed tests usually take place on a closed course. The cars are driven much faster than a person would usually drive. In this way, carmakers test the vehicle's safety for highway driving.

Drivers take cars over uneven surfaces for **rough-road tests**. These tests show whether the cars will be safe on all kinds of roads.

Wet-road tests make sure cars will be able to drive, turn, and stop safely even on slippery roads.

Companies want to make sure car designs are as safe as possible!

Stopping tests check that the brakes work when cars are driven at different speeds and in different types of weather.

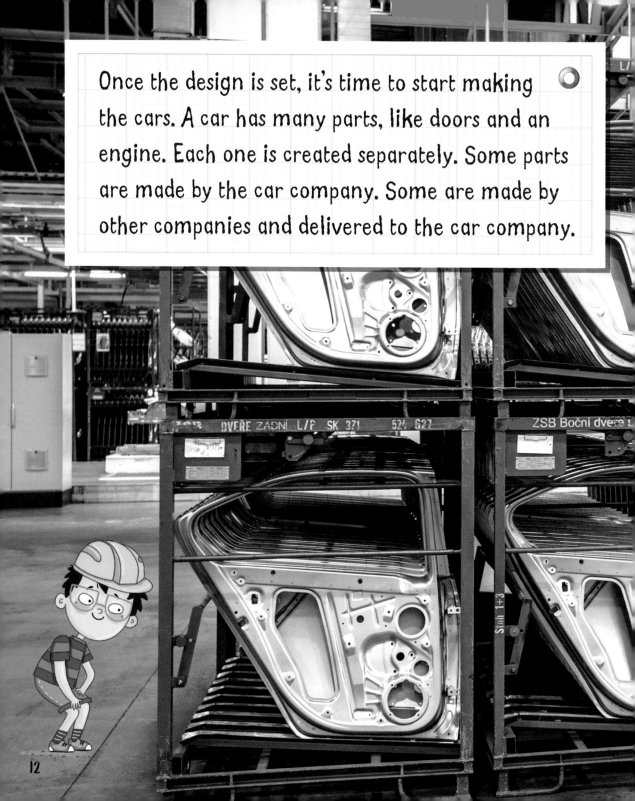

Once the design is set, it's time to start making the cars. A car has many parts, like doors and an engine. Each one is created separately. Some parts are made by the car company. Some are made by other companies and delivered to the car company.

Each part of a car is made of many smaller parts. If you could count every piece down to the smallest screws, there would be about 30,000 parts to a car!

Those are car doors.

Cool!

13

The body, which is the main part of the car, is most often made of steel. Steel is inexpensive, strong, and easy to work with. Here is how the body is built.

1 Steel that will be used to make a car body starts out flat. It arrives at the car factory in big rolls.

2 Next, steel is cut from a sheet. Then it is bent and cut in a machine to make parts like doors, roofs, and hoods.

3 Finally, the different parts are welded together to make the body. Welding is the joining of two pieces of metal by heat. This job is often done by robots!

4 Then the body is ready for the next step!

Robots . . . Cool!

Welding can be dangerous work for people. That is why robots usually do it.

Another important part of a car is the powertrain. The powertrain makes a car move. It includes several different parts. The main one is the engine. It provides the power used to turn the wheels.

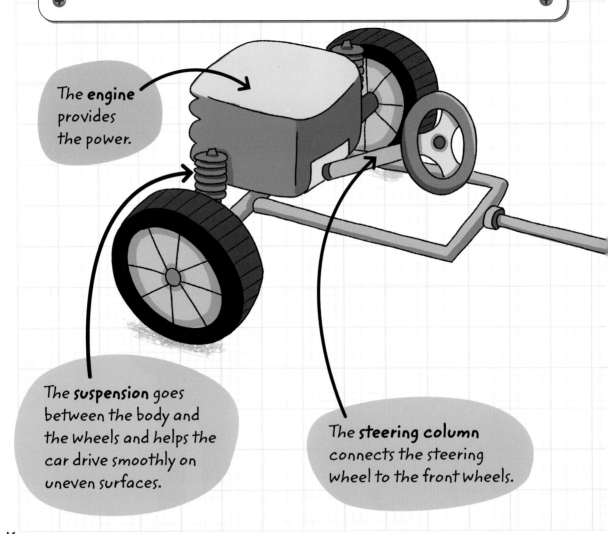

The **engine** provides the power.

The **suspension** goes between the body and the wheels and helps the car drive smoothly on uneven surfaces.

The **steering column** connects the steering wheel to the front wheels.

The **drive shaft** is a rod that helps deliver power from the engine to the rear wheels.

After the powertrain is installed, it will be inspected to make sure there are no problems. In fact, every part of the car is inspected!

A lot of parts work together to make a car move!

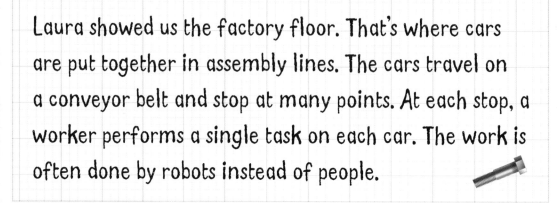

Laura showed us the factory floor. That's where cars are put together in assembly lines. The cars travel on a conveyor belt and stop at many points. At each stop, a worker performs a single task on each car. The work is often done by robots instead of people.

An assembly line lets companies produce a lot of cars in a day.

It would take a lot longer for teams of people to make each car from start to finish.

Henry Ford is credited with introducing the assembly line in car factories. He used it to build the Ford Model T car in 1913.

The last step in making the body of the car is the paint job. Laura showed us how that works.

1

First, the body is washed to clean off any dirt. Then it is passed through a special pool of paint that has electricity flowing through it (called the E-coat), to prevent rust.

2

Next, robots spray on several coats of paint. The first coat keeps the surface smooth. The next coat adds color. A clear coat is added last to make the car shiny.

3 Finally, the paint is dried in a big oven, and then it is cooled.

The most popular car colors in North America are white, black, gray, and silver.

I'd like a red car like this one!

Next, the powertrain is put into the body. And many, many more parts are added to the inside and outside of the car!

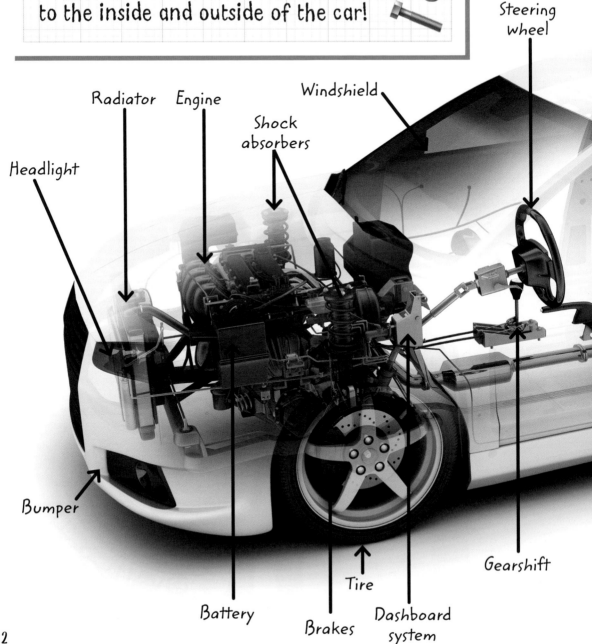

Radiator Engine

Windshield

Steering wheel

Shock absorbers

Headlight

Bumper

Gearshift

Tire

Battery

Brakes

Dashboard system

Gas tank

Exhaust system

Gas cap

Taillight

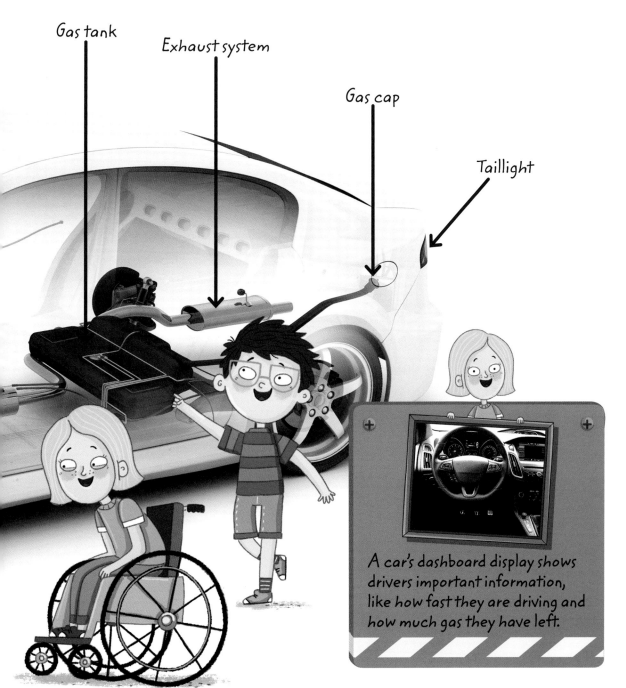

A car's dashboard display shows drivers important information, like how fast they are driving and how much gas they have left.

Once the car is all put together, it is inspected to make sure it works. If anything does not work, it is fixed. Then the car is finished! It's put onto a ship, train, or truck to be taken to a car dealership.

The biggest car carrier ships can hold about 8,000 cars!

In recent years, more than 75 million cars have been produced around the world every year.

The weekend after we visited the factory, my mom took the entire junior engineers club to an auto show. Zoe and I got to show everyone the car model we'd seen built—and lots of other cool vehicles!

MACHINERY AND TOOLS FOR BUILDING A CAR

Conveyor
This kind of machine moves material from place to place in the factory. Conveyor belts or rollers move items in front of workers. An overhead conveyor (pictured) moves items above workers.

Welding Robots
These machines use heat to unite parts.

CNC Machines
These are computer-controlled machine tools that cut or shape metal, wood, plastic, and other hard materials.

Painting Robots
These machines spray on paint quickly and evenly.

Torque Wrench
This wrench is used to tighten fasteners, such as nuts and bolts. It is designed to make the fasteners exactly as tight as they need to be.

Mobile Lift
This machine lifts up the car. That lets workers get to the lower parts and underside of the car more easily.

Rivet Gun
This tool drives rivets. A rivet is a metal pin that fastens two or more items together. After the pin is put through a hole, the end is deformed to keep it in place.

Torque Screwdriver
This tool is designed to turn screws exactly as tight as they need to be.

CARS BUILT IN AMAZING WAYS

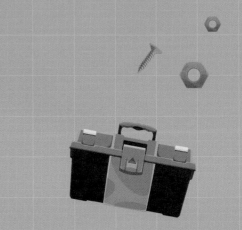

Lunar Roving Vehicle (LRV)
The "moon buggy" was used on American missions to the moon. This vehicle was specially designed to work on the moon's very rough surface and in its low-gravity atmosphere.

Stretch Limousine
Stretch limos are made by cutting an ordinary-size car in half and expanding it! Extra supports are added to make the body so long.

Underwater Car
The Rinspeed sQuba can be driven on land and underwater! It uses three electric motors and has an open top. Passengers breathe underwater with scuba-like tubes.

Self-Driving Cars
These cars use sensors, cameras, and computers to drive by themselves. No humans needed! Self-driving cars are still being developed.

Race Car
Practically every detail of a race car is handmade. Race cars are designed to be driven very hard and fast for a short time. Then they are rebuilt for the next race!

INDEX

ABOUT THE AUTHOR

Becky Herrick is a writer and editor who lives in New Jersey with her husband, daughter, and cat. She loves learning about how things are built!